INTRODUCTION

Austin didn't know what to expect when he sent out a tweet inviting fans to a meetup in Millennium Park (ABOVE).

In October 2011, Austin Mahone was becoming a YouTube sensation. He knew he had at least a few true fans. So he got on Twitter. He let the world know exactly when he'd be at the huge stainless-steel, bean-shaped sculpture in Chicago's Millennium Park, just in case anyone wanted to meet him.

Dressed in a gray hoodie and a red baseball cap, Austin didn't look much different from any other fifteen-year-old. But his fans, called Mahomies, weren't fooled for a minute.

Austin donned an out-of-this-world shirt for a 2013 trip to New York.

Austin smiles for the camera with a young fan.

As soon as the Mahomies spotted him, they swarmed. Screaming fans rushed over, hurdling picnic tables along the way and snapping pics. Police on duty in the park faced a great challenge to reach the center of the scene.

Austin may have expected just a handful of fans, but the crowd he attracted was major. More than one thousand people showed up to see him. It was too much for the police. The meet and greet was officially shut down.

Later that day, Austin took to YouTube. He apologized for the change in plans. He thanked his fans for their support. And with a dazed expression on his face, he commented on the earlier events.

"Crazy. Crazy stuff," he said, smiling and shaking his head. In a soft voice, he shared his feelings openly. **"It's the first time that's ever happened to me.** I was a little scared. It was kind of fun, though. I had a good time."

Mahomie Madness in Chicago - 1000 fans show up at meet and greet for Austin Mahone - vid 2

1:02 / 2:34

full screen

Austin couldn't believe his popularity with his YouTube fans. After the meet and greet in Millennium Park, he knew he could be a star.

Austin and his BFF, Alex Constancio (RIGHT), began working toward their big dreams together.

CHAPTER ONE

CHANNELING FAME

austin mahone and alex constancio dancing

Upload   Sign in

1:05 / 7:15

Austin Mahone & Alex Constancio - Cool Morning 1,2,3

TheSoccer1DGirl   5 videos

58,539

▶ Subscribe   144

👍 770   👎 11

Like

About   Share   Add to

Published on Jul 9, 2013
Cool Morning:)

51 videos   Mix - Austin Mahone & Alex Constancio - Cool Morning 1,2,3
YouTube

البرنامج القوي #elGawee #الزووور
##الموسم_الأول
by elGawee
20:36   249,620   FEATURED

Austin Mahone And Alex Constancio Funny Moments
by Eimantas Kasperavicius
13:30   50,161 views

Austin Mahone (Austream) Dougie with Mama Mahone
by 23UCLAbruin
5:34   154,721 views

Austin Mahone's Best Moments
by ToriandRach1
10:01   431,304 views

Austin Dancing the Dougie with a suprise from his mom!
by 1Mahomie
4:05   69,654 views

Austin Mahone's Best/Cute/Funny Moments [PART 1]
by Michelle McLaren
11:53   46,238 views

Elevator Music
by Alex Mahone

Austin raps with Alex (LEFT) on YouTube.

In 2010, Austin Mahone's name wasn't known around the world. He wasn't even famous in La Vernia, Texas, where he lived with his mom. That summer, though, Austin and his bestie, Alex Constancio, started making YouTube videos together. They danced hip-hop, lip-synched songs, performed skits, and acted out scenes from movies.

Was it just for kicks? No way. The pair had bigger dreams and tried to make fame part of the equation. They posted links to their MySpace and Facebook pages. They printed fliers advertising their videos and passed them out at the mall. In these ways, Austin and Alex managed to get their names out to lots of people.

FAMILY MATTERS

Austin lives with his mom, Michele, who is also his manager. He is an only child.

Austin, a seventh grader, plays it cool before the camera.

Going Solo

A few months later, in January 2011, Austin struck out on his own as a musical artist. He created another YouTube channel where he strummed the guitar and crooned covers. He performed songs by popular artists such as Justin Bieber and Jason Mraz.

Austin set himself apart from others who sang on YouTube by giving his fans something more: personal attention.

click to play all my vids

ck to subscribe(:

Austin wanted to share some of his favorite songs with YouTube fans on his own channel.

When Austin was six, he saw a drum set for sale in a local music store. He convinced his mom to buy it for him. He then taught himself to play, and his love of music was set in stone.

Whenever someone commented on one of Austin's performances, he replied with a comment of his own. Hearing from the artist drew people in. That meant not just more views and comments but more subscribers too. After only two months, the unknown kid from La Vernia had twenty thousand subscribers to his channel. Those people were automatically informed every time Austin posted a new video.

Austin was born in San Antonio, Texas, on April 4, 1996.

New Kid on the Scene

In the spring, Austin and his mom moved to San Antonio, Texas. That made Austin the new kid at the local high school. But by then, he was no longer an unfamiliar face. His fellow students acted like paparazzi. **"People were taking pictures of me from behind in class and getting me to talk to their friends on the phone,"** Austin said.

PAPARAZZI =
photographers who chase celebrities to take pictures to sell to magazines and newspapers

Less than one week after he enrolled, Austin opted for homeschooling instead. Without his old friends nearby, he was alone a lot. But he quickly settled into a routine: schoolwork first, then music, and then social media to connect with fans. When he needed to get out, he didn't go far. Usually, he just hit the driveway to shoot some hoops.

Austin was starting to realize he had put his dreams in motion. Life after YouTube would never be the same.

Austin began taking his YouTube act to the stage as his fan base grew.

Austin's mom (RIGHT) helped him a lot as he became a famous singer.

CHAPTER TWO

BREAKING OUT

Austin performed live for iHeartRadio in August 2012.

Austin's first live shows were performed at private parties. In fall 2011, he was hired to play at a party in Chicago, Illinois. The pay: $2,000. And since he was in town, he thought it would be cool to meet some fans in Millennium Park the next day. That's when he found out just how famous he'd become.

The crowd of Mahomies who showed up proved his career was in high gear. Soon after, Austin's mom quit her job as a mortgage loan officer. She became Austin's full-time manager instead, answering e-mails, handling his schedule, shooting videos, and fielding calls from everyone who wanted to work with him.

INSIDE AUSTIN'S ROOM

When Austin first moved to San Antonio, he and his mom stayed with his grandparents. Austin had a tiny bedroom there. He dressed it up with the following:
- Tons of fan mail
- Framed posters of Michael Jordan and Justin Bieber
- Gifts from fans—such as a plaster bust of his own head

PARTY ANIMAL—NOT!

When Austin turned sixteen, he celebrated in low-key style with old friends. They dined at the Olive Garden and then hit a local bowling alley.

Kickin' It Up a Notch

In April 2012, Austin signed with the management group Chase Entertainment. Now, he had an entire team of people to help him become a superstar. Soon after, he and his mom made another move.

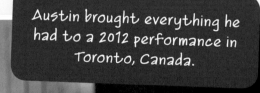

Austin brought everything he had to a 2012 performance in Toronto, Canada.

Austin breaks out his moves at the 2013 Jingle Ball Kickoff Party in New York.

This time, they headed to Miami, Florida, where Austin could perfect his talents. He worked with a vocal coach and a dance instructor and even learned how to field questions from the media.

By May, he was ready to perform live in Philadelphia, Pennsylvania, at the Q102 Springle Ball.

MEDIA =
television, radio, magazines, and other methods of distributing information

Austin was a hit at the Springle Ball in Philadelphia.

The lineup included music sensations Carly Rae Jepsen, Cody Simpson, and Flo Rida. By the summer, entertainment industry experts thought Austin could earn as much as $50,000 per performance—twenty-five times what he made playing at parties!

Label Maker

Without a record label behind him, though, Austin wasn't likely to make it big as a musician. Or was he?

RECORD LABEL =
a company that produces, distributes, and promotes music

Austin had 1.8 million "Likes" on Facebook. He had 1.5 million Twitter followers. And his YouTube channel had 545,000 subscribers. When he released his first original single, "11:11," it was an instant hit with his many fans. It even made *Billboard*'s Heatseekers Songs, a chart that tracks popular songs from artists who have not been in the top 50 of the Hot 100 chart.

TEETH IN TRAINING

Austin wasn't born with a picture-perfect smile. He wore braces until just before the 2012 Q102 Springle Ball.

allyson6679
Cute

acm_central
Plugs not drugs!

helnt__
I LOVEEEE THIS PHOTO♥ OMG U ARE PERFECT!|♥|♥|♥ @austinmahone

treasure_swims
This is the best photo ever. No joke!

gabrielamelim
Perfect

laxmin98
Your welcome! @russellsidhu #doppelganger

russellsidhu
@laxmin98 in which world. Really haha

dmsv_
GUAPISIMOOOOOOOOO!!!

ve a comment...

Austin shares his smile—braces and all—on Instagram.

PICK ME!

Austin continued Skyping with female fans even after he achieved superstardom. He'd pick a caller at random and spend screen time chatting, singing, and strumming his guitar.

By August 2012, Austin's career was on fire. It was time for another life-changing move. He signed with Chase Records and started working on his first full-length album. While he was busy recording with rapper Flo Rida and music producer RedOne, the media couldn't resist making comparisons.

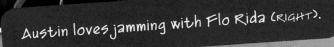

Austin loves jamming with Flo Rida (RIGHT).

Even before his album was out, people started calling Austin the next Justin Bieber.

There was no doubt about it. Austin was now a major figure in the music world.

Austin sent his love to all his fans at a 2012 concert.

PRICEY POP STAR

Austin worked hard to build his fan base on his own. That made him worth more to the many labels that wanted him. Because of that, his management team asked for a deal with Chase Records worth an estimated $3 to $4 million.

One of Austin's Mahomies shared a YouTube video of his 2013 White House performance.

Acoustic Performance Austin
Mahone White House Easter Egg
by TheMahomies
5:49   2,911 views

CHAPTER THREE

RISING STAR

Demi Lovato (LEFT) and Austin (RIGHT) have more than just music in common. They both grew up in Texas!

In 2013, rubbing elbows with stars was an everyday event for Austin. In March, he performed at a Texas rodeo with singer Demi Lovato. In April, he performed at the White House's Easter Egg Roll for President Barack Obama and thousands of guests. In May, he sat next to recording artist Akon and presented an award with singer Kelly Rowland at the Billboard Music Awards.

During the summer, Austin went on tour as an opening act for Taylor Swift. Hanging with an experienced superstar definitely had some perks. Austin got to play for crowds of thousands.

SPREADING THE LOVE

Austin uses his celeb status to support charities including the Muscular Dystrophy Association, the Ryan Seacrest Foundation, the Salvation Army, and the T. J. Martell Foundation.

When he's not singing or playing guitar, Austin likes to play football and basketball.

He got some great advice about staying grounded. And Taylor even tried to set him up with her pretty and talented pal Selena Gomez.

Down but Not Out

Austin's work ethic was off the charts. Some days he got up at three in the morning. He sometimes skipped sleep for almost twenty-four hours. His efforts seemed to be paying off when he won two major music honors.

Austin hung out with Taylor Swift (RIGHT) at the 2013 MTV Video Music Awards.

Austin has a collection of about 150 pairs of shoes. Favorites include Versace shoes he purchased for the Billboard Music Awards and his Nike Air Yeezy II sneakers.

He was named Breakout Artist at the Young Hollywood Awards and Artist to Watch at the MTV Video Music Awards. Austin was excited to headline his own MTV Artist to Watch Tour in the fall. The shows sold out in no time. But then, in October, he posted a photo of himself on Instagram. He was surrounded by medical equipment, wearing a hospital gown, and looking exhausted. The caption read, **"I've never felt so bad."** His lack of sleep and frantic lifestyle had caught up with him.

HEADLINE =
to perform as the main act

Austin was treated for a blood clot in his throat and severe dehydration. The good news was he was going to be fine. The bad news was he had to postpone his tour. He worried about disappointing his fans. But he was in no shape to hit the road.

FAN FAVORITE

In 2014, Austin had 7 million Facebook "Likes," 5 million Twitter followers, and 1 million YouTube subscribers.

Forward Thinking

Getting back on track didn't take Austin long. By the end of October, he had rescheduled his tour dates for the next year. In December, he performed in a series of Jingle Ball concerts that took him all around the country. He also kept working hard on his debut album. Before releasing it, he wanted to make sure every song was just right.

DEBUT =
first album or performance for the public

One thing was for sure. Austin would continue making a name for himself as a musical artist no one could forget. Mahomies were eagerly awaiting Austin's next moves too.

Austin performs in style at Jingle Ball 2013 in Miami.

Austin high-fives one of his fans at Planet Hollywood in New York.

AUSTIN
PICS!

Austin knows how to have fun on the stage and on the red carpet.

Austin shows off some slick hip-hop moves at Jingle Ball 2013 in St. Paul, Minnesota.

SOURCE NOTES

7   "Mahomie Madness in Chicago—1000 Fans Show Up at Meet and Greet for Austin Mahone—Vid 2," YouTube video, 0:12, posted by "Austin Mahone," October 23, 2011, http://www.youtube.com/watch?v=R7xlpKgvIRg.

12   Jenny Eliscu, "The Making of Baby Bieber: How Austin Mahone Is Riding Social Media to Superstardom," *Hollywood Reporter*, June 6, 2012, http://www.hollywoodreporter.com/news/austin-mahone-justin-bieber-youtube-sensation-333443.

26   Austin Mahone, *Instagram*, October 17, 2013, http://instagram.com/austinmahone.

MORE AUSTIN INFO

Austin Mahone: Startin' Something Spectacular. Chicago: Triumph Books, 2013. Read up on Austin's life before fame.

Austin's Facebook Page
https://www.facebook.com/AustinMahone
If you're a Facebook user, be Austin's newest friend!

Austin's Instagram Page
http://instagram.com/AustinMahone#
Check out Austin's latest pics.

Austin's Twitter Page
https://twitter.com/AustinMahone
Get the latest Austin news—straight from the singer himself!

Austin's YouTube Page
https://www.youtube.com/user/AustinMahone
Watch Austin sing and dance on the site that jump-started his stardom.

INDEX

The images in this book are used with the permission of: © Noam Galai/WireImage/Getty Images, pp. 2, 23; © Uri Schanker/FilmMagic/Getty Images, pp. 3 (top), 13; © Brian Hineline/Retna Ltd., pp. 3 (bottom), 18; © C Flanigan/FilmMagic/Getty Images, p. 4 (upper left); © Adam Bettcher /Getty Images Entertainment/Getty Images, pp. 4 (upper right), 29 (lower left); © Lissandra Melo /Shutterstock.com, p. 4 (bottom); © D Dipasupil/Getty Images Entertainment/Getty Images, p. 5; © Larry Marano/Getty Images Entertainment/Getty Images, pp. 6, 11, 20, 27; Courtesy YouTube, pp. 7, 8, 10, 22 (top); © Michael Buckner/Getty Images Entertainment/Getty Images, p. 8 (top); Seth Poppel Yearbook Library, p. 9; © Jo Ann Snover/Shutterstock.com, p. 12; © Bruce Glikas /FilmMagic/Getty Images, p. 14 (top); © Scott Weiner/Retna Ltd./CORBIS, p. 14 (bottom); © C Flanigan/WireImage/Getty Images, p. 15; © Sonia Recchia/WireImage/Getty Images, p. 16; © Brock Miller/Splash News/CORBIS, p. 17; Courtesy of Austin Mahone via Instagram, pp. 19, 26; © Eugene Gologursky/WireImage/Getty Images, p. 21; © Aaron Davidson/WireImage/Getty Images, p. 22 (bottom left); Jerry Lara/ZUMA Press/Newscom, p. 22 (bottom right); © Kevin Mazur/WireImage/Getty Images, p. 24; Dee Cercone/Courtesy Everett Collection, p. 25; © Bruce Glikas/FilmMagic/Getty Images, p. 28 (top left); © Paul Warner/WireImage/Getty Images, p. 28 (bottom left); © Joe Seer/Shutterstock.com, p. 28 (right); © Rick Diamond/Getty Images Entertainment/Getty Images, p. 29 (top left); © Brian Patterson Photos/Shutterstock.com, p. 29 (right).

Front Cover: © Alexander Tamargo/Getty Images Entertainment/Getty Images; Ouzounova/Splash News/Newscom (top left).
Back Cover: © Paul Warner/WireImage/Getty Images.

Main body text set in Shannon Std Book 12/18.
Typeface provided by Monotype Typography.

POP CULTURE BIOS

AUSTIN

MAHONE

VOCALS GOING VIRAL

HEATHER E. SCHWARTZ

Lerner Publications Company

MINNEAPOLIS

Lerner Publications Company
A division of Lerner Publishing Group, Inc.
241 First Avenue North
Minneapolis, MN 55401 USA

For reading levels and more information, look up this title at
www.lernerbooks.com.

Library of Congress Cataloging-in-Publication Data

Schwartz, Heather E., author.
        Austin Mahone : vocals going viral / by Heather E. Schwartz.
          pages   cm. — (Pop culture bios)
        Includes index.
        ISBN 978-1-4677-3670-1 (lib. bdg. : alk. paper)
        ISBN 978-1-4677-4731-8 (eBook)
        1. Mahone, Austin, 1996- —Juvenile literature.
     2. Singers—United States—Biography—Juvenile literature.
     I. Title.
     ML3930.M27S38 2015
     782.42164092—dc23 [B]   2013050212

Manufactured in the United States of America
1 – PC – 7/15/14